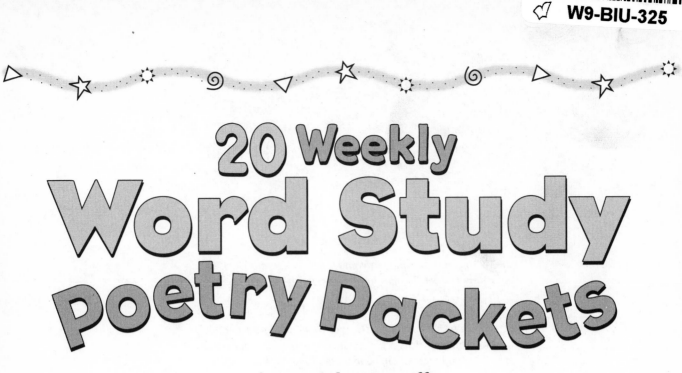

20 Weekly Word Study Poetry Packets

by Janiel Wagstaff

SCHOLASTIC
PROFESSIONAL BOOKS

New York • Toronto • London • Auckland • Sydney
Mexico City • New Delhi • Hong Kong • Buenos Aires

Dedication

To my niece Lily Cate who loves sign-songing . . .
May your life be filled with magic and poetry!

Acknowledgements:

My sincerest gratitude to Wendy Murray, Joanna Davis-Swing,
and Terry Cooper for allowing me to publish my first book of poetry!

Thanks Mom and Dad, as always.

Thanks Mr. Johnson (Husbee Broom) for your photos,
your drawing skills, your classroom assistance, your patience,
and most of all, your sense of humor. I love you!

Thanks to my students and great friends at Creekside Elementary
for making every day a fun day to teach and learn.

For information regarding literacy workshops presented by Janiel Wagstaff, contact:
Institute for Enrichment in Education
Phone: (801) 546-6009   Fax: (801) 546-4053

Cover design by Maria Lilja
Cover artwork by Peggy Tagel
Interior design by Sydney Wright
Interior artwork by Stephen Lewis

ISBN: 0-439-37654-8
Copyright © 2003 by Janiel Wagstaff

3 4 5 6 7 8 9 10   40   09 08 07 06 05 04 03

Contents

Introduction

This book is much more than another collection of poems, rhymes, and chants. Every rhyme was written to connect with early childhood curriculum, and each is accompanied by corresponding word work activities for teaching and reinforcing phonics. Grouping these activities together saves time and makes your job easier.

I've produced this volume because I believe it best to integrate our instruction by making as many connections across disciplines as possible. The individual rhymes relate to curriculum areas and provide a way to reinforce reading throughout the day. In addition, the rhymes are directly related to all word work activities. Not only does this process save instructional time (for example, you can teach reading concepts while working with a science poem), but students also benefit from viewing reading, writing, spelling, and word work as interrelated. They come to understand how activity in one area is relevant to another.

Another benefit to this approach is it saves lesson preparation time. It is no longer necessary to find something for shared reading, something for phonemic awareness, something else for independent reading, something else for spelling and maybe even something else for word work. The rhymes, Practice Pages, Word Sorts, and Word Scrambles can be used for all of these. You can delve into science, social studies, math, and other content, too, since the rhymes have cross-curricular themes. Any tool that helps meet these needs is worth looking into. Consider how:

* *The poems, rhymes, and chants are a source of shared reading*

   I write them on chart paper and mount them on chart stands. At the beginning of the week, we read the chart together in a shared reading

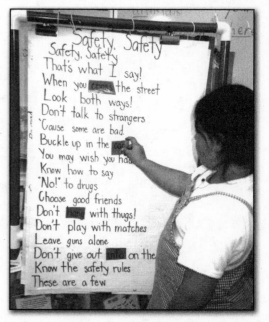

▲ *A student uses highlighting tape to harvest key words.*

format. We revisit the shared reading chart frequently for choral rereadings. For example, we reread the chart before our word work each day. Students reread independently or in pairs from the shared reading charts as they "read the room." We also reread together before related science, social studies, or math activities. I take advantage of all opportunities to make connections back to the poems, rhymes, or chants.

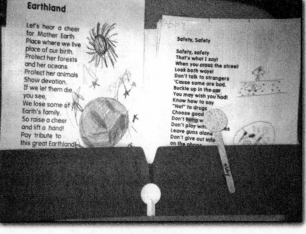

▲ *A Favorites Folder*

✳ *The poems, rhymes, and chants are sources of independent reading*

Later in the week (Wednesday or Thursday), I give the kids a copy of the "favorite" (that's what we call the new rhyme, poem, or chant of the week) to keep in their Favorites Folders (two-pocket portfolios). Since we have repeatedly read the favorite together in a shared reading format, students experience success when they reread it independently or with a buddy. Of course, repeated readings from the Favorites Folder boost fluency and automaticity, too.

✳ *The poems, Practice Pages, and Word Scrambles boost phonological awareness*

All of the favorites rhyme. After hearing the poem read aloud or during shared reading, the class can round up the rhyming words *orally* as one way to build phonological awareness. The Practice Pages help students hear and manipulate sounds while making connections between words. This is all done *orally* before any words are written. Both of these activities help to tune students in to listening for and comparing sound units inside words. Additionally, the "push the sounds" component of the Word Scrambles heightens phonological awareness as students segment words into parts and blend the parts back together.

✳ *The Practice Pages, Word Sorts, and Word Scrambles fill the need for phonics and spelling practice*

The Practice Pages, Word Sorts, and Word Scrambles are based on key words contained in the poems, rhymes, and chants. Practice Pages and Word Sorts provide practice with common spelling patterns (phonograms, rimes, or chunks)

Fluency: smooth, accurate, effortless reading. Fluent readers use appropriate speed and expression; their reading sounds like talking. Nonfluent readers have trouble with word recognition and phrasing; they read choppily.

Automaticity: automatic, effortless word recognition.

Phonological Awareness: the understanding that spoken language is made up of units of sound (including words, syllables, onsets and rimes, and phonemes) and the ability to distinguish and manipulate these sound units (as with orally blending sounds together to make words and taking words apart by orally segmenting their sounds).

▲ *A student works on a word scramble activity.*

and analogous spelling words. Word Scrambles enable students to analyze words all the way down to the phoneme level as they mix and reassemble letter cards.

These activities help with decoding, too. As students reread the Practice Pages, they practice decoding a related list of words. For example, they may read, "The key word is *dressed*. It has the *ess* chunk. So these must be *bless*, *stress*, and *messy*." After students sort the words in the Word Sort, they are asked to decode analogous words in the categories before clean-up. Mixing and reassembling letter cards during the Word Scrambles enriches students' abilities to segment words into sounds and blend those sounds back together to create words (both critical to decoding and spelling).

✳ *The Word Wall and additional word work activities spring from the poems, rhymes, and chants*

The words we study from the rhymes, practice on the Practice Pages, and manipulate in the Word Sorts and Word Scrambles are the *same* key words that are posted on the Word Wall. Since they are the same words, taken from meaningful contexts and referred to and practiced in multiple ways, students really do learn them and commit them to memory. This approach makes having and using a classroom Word Wall more successful.

✳ *The Word Sorts and Practice Pages give students practice with words beyond those on the Word Wall or in the rhymes*

As students fill in the Practice Pages, multiple examples are generated for each key word. Students hear and spell many analogous words beyond the one key word for the Word Wall. Likewise, the Word Sorts encourage students to go beyond the key words from the rhymes or poems by sorting and reading a number of new analogous words. These activities are powerful because they emphasize the connections between

▲ *A student reads a practice page and generates additional words that contain the chunk from the key word.*

words. Since many different words are generated during this word work, the activities lend themselves to incidental vocabulary instruction as the class discusses word meanings.

* *The poems, rhymes, and chants can fit into your spelling program*

There are several ways you might fit the key words into your spelling program. First, you might limit your spelling words to just the key words of the week, if appropriate. Or, make your list consist of the key words plus an appropriate number and type (simple, complex/single syllable, multisyllabic) of analogous words. If you have a required spelling program, just add the key words of the week to the list. If this makes too many words, cut out some of the required program words (usually these lists contain several examples of the same rule or pattern—cut out some of the redundant examples). In my second-grade classroom, we use the key words of the week and add our "very own words" from writing workshop drafts. This results in individualized student lists. We buddy up on Friday to take spelling tests so if students forget any of their "very own words," buddies can read them from their list.

Determining if and how to compose and use a spelling list is just one aspect of an effective spelling program. Combining a list approach with use of the Word Wall, interrelated word work activities, and daily process writing, helps students truly grow as spellers!

* *The poems, rhymes, and chants relate to multiple content areas*

The "favorites" in this volume are some of my most useful resources for teaching and reinforcing varied content area concepts. They are fun and educational. Many contain important vocabulary and lend themselves to song or movement. For example, I wrote "Insects, Insects" when teaching about insects in science. The poem provided me with the opportunity to clarify concepts and was a springboard for many student-generated questions that led to research.

As you can see, many connections are possible with the resources in this book. I actually fought the idea of publishing them based on my belief that teachers should find their own favorites related to what they are teaching, and involve the students in picking the key words (Wagstaff, 1999; 1994). Given our busy schedules, however, I know this ideal is not always possible. Furthermore, I've noticed how I use some favorites year after year with great success. Teachers in my workshops have repeatedly asked for these resources, as well. So here they are! It's been a great help to me to put them together in one place and I'm sure they'll prove useful to you!

—*Janiel Wagstaff*

How will this fit in with my reading program?
Because there are so many reading programs out there and schools frequently change their program, I have developed methods and materials that are universal. They can be integrated into any reading program, but most importantly, they are sound instructionally and fun, too! This book contains some of my best resources for integrating reading and word work into the total curriculum. I use the big books, charts, copies of small books, and anthologies of stories from our reading program as resources for shared, guided, and independent reading and writing. I build the required program's resources into the total curriculum instead of building the curriculum around these resources.

CHAPTER 1

Using the Poems, Rhymes, Chants, and Word Work Activities in Your Classroom

Each poem, rhyme, or chant is followed by three accompanying word work activities: a Word Scramble, a Practice Page, and a Word Sort (see pages 17–20 for an example of a packet). Each packet can be completed in a week; however, this time frame may be adjusted to fit the needs of your students. Since each poem, rhyme, or chant relates to the total curriculum, you may choose to teach the packet as the topic occurs in your schedule. For example, I often begin the year with the poem and word work activities for "If You Think You Know This Friend" since we are working with names and "Get to Know You" activities during the first week of school. During the week when Earth Day occurs, we complete the packet for "Earthland"; just as we do "A Brand-new Year" to ring in each New Year in January and complete "Adding Is Fun" and "When You Need to Subtract" when working on carrying and borrowing in math.

A Weekly Schedule

The following is the weekly schedule I use to integrate the rhymes, poems, chants, and word work into my literacy program. The schedule is the same regardless of grade level since it rests on the same philosophy. That is:

1. **Monday: Capture the students' attention and motivation with a fun poem, rhyme, or chant.** Get them excited about the curriculum you'll be studying by emphasizing the content in the rhymes. (For example, when using the "Insects, Insects" poem, I started the week by bringing in my bug collection and showing the kids how we would be making our own terrariums for collecting and observing live insects).

2. Monday: Harvest key words from the rhyme.

3. Tuesday–Thursday: Read and reread the poem, rhyme, or chant to support reading success.

4. Tuesday–Thursday: Reinforce and practice the key words throughout the week using the Word Scrambles, Practice Pages, and Word Sorts.

5. Friday: Post the key words on a Word Wall, and refer to them all year.

❶ Capture students' attention and motivation with a fun poem, rhyme, or chant.

Introduce the rhyme in a shared reading format on a chart or overhead. With the youngest students, you may teach the rhyme orally first. For older students, as the year progresses and students become more fluent, you might introduce the rhyme by simply handing out copies. This way, everyone can read it independently first, then chorally as a class. You can discuss any difficulties encountered while reading and the strategies used to overcome them.

❷ Harvest key words from the rhyme.

Each poem contains three to five key words for weekly study. I used high-frequency chunk lists and my own testing to choose the words most useful to students. If you use every packet in the book, you'll have taught 85 important chunks! You will find the key words for each selection following the copy of the poem at the top of the Word Scrambles and Word Sorts and down the left side of the Practice Pages.

▲ *Harvested words from a poem.*

After reading and rereading the selection, "harvest" the key Word Wall words by asking volunteers to highlight these words on the chart or overhead with Wikki stix or highlighting tape (see page 4). Write the key words on cards. Use Stick-e-tak to post the word cards on the chalkboard for practice throughout the week (see right). At the end of the week, once the key words are familiar, add them to the classroom Word Wall.

❸ Read and reread the poem, rhyme, or chant to support reading success.

Each day, we do a shared rereading of the favorite—sing it, act it out, and so on—before we move into word work. Students are given a copy on Wednesday or Thursday (depending on which seems appropriate based on their degree of reading success). They use a highlighting pen to highlight the key words of the week on their copy. Then they add the copy to their two-pocket portfolio—Favorites Folder—and get together with a neighbor to read, sing, and act out previous favorites.

❹ *Reinforce and practice the key words throughout the week.*

Once you've highlighted the key words from the rhyme, poem, or chant, students need multiple opportunities to really *learn them*. They also need plenty of chances to *use them* to read and write new words. Those are the goals of the word work activities, which I've categorized as Word Scrambles, Practice Pages, and Word Sorts.

We generally complete Word Scrambles on Tuesdays, Practice Pages on Wednesdays, and Word Sorts on Thursdays.

Using the Word Scrambles

This activity is like the make-and-break word work in Reading Recovery (Clay, 1993). The key words for the week are formatted in boxes for Word Scrambling (see page 18 for an example). Students cut the letter boxes for each word, then mix the letters and re-form the word (using the desk or floor). Each word is mixed and made at least three times. Next, students "push the sounds." This activity allows practice in analyzing the sounds in words by segmenting then blending. I begin this process by modeling how to break the key words into beginning letters (onsets) and chunks (rimes) (see box at left). The letters of the onset are then pushed upward together while the sound is voiced. The letters of the rime are

▲ *A student "pushes the sounds."*

next pushed upward together while the chunk is voiced. Then, students run their index fingers under the word, blending the sounds together to read the word. "Push the sounds" is also repeated three times.

Once students are skilled at segmenting and blending words at the onset and rime level, teach them how to listen deeper inside words to "push the sounds" at the phoneme level. Students push each letter or letter combination representing each phoneme upward while voicing each sound one after the other. Then they run their index fingers under the word, blending the sounds together to read the word. This procedure is repeated three times.

Onsets and **rimes** are parts of the syllables within words. The *onset* is the consonant or consonant cluster before the vowel and the *rime* is the vowel and the letters that come after (the rhyming part of the syllable). For example, in the word *toothpick*, there are two syllables. The onset in the first syllable is *t*, the rime is *ooth*. The onset in the second syllable is *p*, the rime is *ick*. Not all syllables have an onset, but they always have a rime.

Troubleshooting

When working on the Word Scrambles, how do you push the sounds at the phoneme level when there is more than one letter card representing the individual sound (like s and h for /sh/) or when there is a silent letter (like e in white)?

Think of using the Word Scrambles just like magnetic letters or letter tiles. When "pushing the sounds" of phonemes represented by more than one letter, simply use two fingers to push the two letters upward at the same time, while voicing the one sound. If the word contains a silent letter, push the letter together with the following (or preceding) letter. For example, when pushing the sounds in the word *white*, use two fingers to push *w* and *h* upward at the same time while voicing /w/, then push the *i* upward while voicing /i/, then push the *t* and *e* upward together while voicing /t/. Remember to follow up by running a finger under and blending the parts together to read the word.

By having to push more than one letter card at the same time to represent one sound, students get the idea that words are often written with more letters than there are sounds. This is an important spelling concept!

You might give students the option to use the letter cards to create other words once they have finished their required Word Scramble activities. New words can be recorded on paper and turned in for credit. The letter cards may also be taken home in an envelope for more practice.

Having the ready-made Word Scrambles has been very useful in my teaching. Prior to developing this idea, when I wanted students to "mix and make" and push the sounds we used magnetic letters and worked in small groups (since I didn't have enough magnetic letters for everyone in the class) or we had to find and distribute the right letter cards. Now it's much easier because the letters needed for the activity are right there on the page. No management of magnets or letter cards is needed; I just pass out the Word Scramble and everyone is ready to go!

Using the Practice Pages

The Practice Pages (see sample at right) are designed to promote automaticity with chunks and to allow students to apply the analogy strategies (see box on page 12) as

▲ *Practice Page for "Colors."*

they make connections between words. ("If I know *dressed*, these are *bless*, *stress*, and *messy*.") I list the words of the week on the left side, underlining each chunk. Together, the students and I orally generate analogous words with the same chunk. I give words for them to try, and allow students to volunteer words. We record three or four of these underneath each key word. I model the correct spelling of analogous words on the overhead or chalkboard since I want to be sure students are recording them correctly on their Practice Pages. I also circulate around the room, specifically checking on more needy students, to make certain the words are correct.

Troubleshooting

What if the students and I have a hard time coming up with analogous words to write on the Practice Pages?

As you work on the Practice Pages, at times, you might get stuck trying to think of analogous words for students to write. The kids are usually very good at this, but sometimes they offer only simple, single-syllable words and you want to stretch their skills further. If stuck, look at the accompanying Word Sort for the week. Remember, the Word Sorts are in essence lists of analogous words, so there will be many right there at your fingertips!

While generating analogous words to write under the key words, what do you do if students offer words that have the right sound but a different spelling for the chunk?

When this happens, congratulate the student for coming up with an analogous word, and model how some chunks have more than one spelling. For example, if the key word is *dare* with the *are* chunk, a student might volunteer the word *where*. I respond with something like, "You're right! *Where* does have the same sound as the *are* chunk in *dare*. But in the word *where*, it is spelled differently. (I write the word *where* on the board in brackets and underline the spelling of its chunk). See? Some chunks have more than one spelling. We'll only write the words with the same spelling as the key words on our Practice Pages."

> "Analogy strategies" is a term I use to refer to *decoding and spelling* new words based on making connections to known words. For example, if students know the key words *shock* and *wing*, they can read or write the new related word *stocking* by hearing the connections between the words and using their common spelling patterns.

On the right side of the Practice Pages, I provide sentences and pictures using the key words. These are meant to be reminders if students get stuck while rereading. They fold the paper on the dotted line and practice reading the key words, chunks, and analogous words. If they need help, they turn the paper over for the context clues. Students can read and reread the pages on their own or with a partner. Partners might take turns being "the teacher" who points to the words, and "the student" who reads the words.

Practice Pages may be sent home for review and brought back to school. They accumulate throughout the year in our Practice Folders (two-pocket portfolios) and are quickly reviewed each week as new pages are added. We might even read from our folders for a few minutes as a word study activity on another day of the week. Practice Page rereading sessions are very brief, lasting only four or five minutes. Students like to challenge themselves to see how many pages they can work through during that time. As they work through the pages, they can see how their word-reading skills are improving and they often want to show off for others (send the Practice Folder home for a night for a quick celebration of their success).

We use special pointers to reread the pages. At the beginning of the school year, we glue buttons or felt pieces on craft sticks and Velcro them inside our Practice Folders. This handy trick keeps our pointers right where we need them!

Using the Ready-made Word Sorts

I always liked the idea of sorting words for sounds and spelling patterns. My problem as a teacher was preparation time. I never seemed to have time to write the words on cards for us to sort. So I started generating the sorts on the computer. Now I format them so they are multilevel and can be used with students of different abilities. Additionally, I put the words on the page in columns so they are easy for kids to cut and sort.

Each sort is based on the same key words taken from the poems, studied on the Practice Pages and Word Scrambles and posted on the Word Wall. Key words are positioned at the top of each page in the largest font with the chunks underlined. Analogous words are listed in columns beginning with the easiest words at top. Words become progressively harder down the columns. This way, teachers can copy the page and individualize by cutting away the bottom columns to make the task easier for some students (see sample at right). Additionally, the multilevel nature of the sorts makes each useful at any grade level. First-grade teachers, for example, may cut away the bottom columns of a more complex sort before copying to make it easier for their students.

When introducing the sorts, demonstrate how to easily cut out the words by beginning at the bottom of the page and cutting upward on the dotted line to reveal

Word Sort for "Animal Voices"

fish	blub
hiss	cat
duck	

cub	wish	pat
bats	kisses	luck
rub	buck	sub
dishes	chat	fatter
missed	swish	tuck
truck	bliss	splat
hissing	lucky	club
flatten	grub	stuck
struck	dismiss	buckle
bubble	Saturday	fishes

▲ *Word Sort for "Animal Voices."*

each column. Taking each column, cut the words horizontally into small, individual word cards.

▲ *A student cuts apart words for a Word Sort.*

Students sort the cards in categories under the larger key words. They use their desktops or the floor. When individuals complete their sort, they begin working on their "punch cards" (Opitz and Ford, 2001). The punch card lists a variety of reading and writing activities for students to choose from. Materials for the activities are stored in bins. Each activity is carefully modeled when it is introduced so students are able to work independently. When I see an individual doing a punch card activity, I ask him/her to show me the sort; I quickly check it, and randomly choose some words for the student to read aloud.

Troubleshooting

What if students have trouble decoding the analogous words?

I help them make connections to the key words at the top of the columns by saying something like, "If the word you know is _____ (pointing to the key word at the top of the column), then this word must be_____." If this prompting does not work, I cover up the chunk(s) in the word and have the student decode the onset first, then the rime, then blend them together. If a word is multisyllabic, I use my finger to cover parts of the word so that just one chunk shows at a time. These tricks really work and they reinforce the analogy strategy for students who are struggling.

Some additional side benefits from the Words Sorts include:

* vocabulary exposure: as kids read the analogous words after sorting, they often ask one another what words mean. You can capitalize on this by writing challenging words on the board and reviewing their meanings with the class. You might also copy a Word Sort onto an overhead, cut it up, and model sorting and reading while explaining new vocabulary.

* work with prefixes and suffixes: while completing the different sorts, your students while come across several common prefixes and suffixes over and over. These include: *un-, -ed, -ing, -ly, -est, -er, -s, -es,* and *-ful.* Make sure to visit this as a teaching point, modeling how words can "grow" when different beginnings and endings are added.

Extending the Use of the Word Sorts

Each student is handed an envelope to store cards after the sort is checked. I place four or five of these completed envelopes in a tote tray labeled "Word Sorts" for future sorting in centers or choice activities. One option is to file the rest in a folder where a copy of the related favorite and Practice Page is also kept. This way, the sorts can be used again, even in subsequent school years.

Another idea is to send the word cards home in the envelope for sorting homework. Teach the children to fold a paper into columns, gluing the larger key words at the top. Students then re-sort the cards and glue them in the appropriate columns. They might even add analogous words of their own at the end of the categories. The paper is turned in for homework credit, and the envelope can be returned to use again.

⑤ *Post the key words on a Word Wall, and continue to refer to them all year.*

▲ *On Fridays, volunteers place the key words in their proper places on the classroom Word Wall.*

Now that the students have practiced the key words, you're ready to post them on your classroom Word Wall. Taking the key word cards from the chalkboard (where they had been affixed during the week for practice), make a ceremony of adding them to the Word Wall on Fridays. Review the words with students, reading them aloud and orally generating analogous words. Ask the students where each word belongs on the Word Wall. Have volunteers come forward to affix the word cards to the Wall. (We use Stick-e-tak or Velcro so words are moveable.) Remind students that they can refer to the Wall anytime and even take words to their desks if needed. (See Wagstaff, 1999, for ideas on making your Word Walls interactive, meaningful review activities for key words, and on conserving classroom wall space.) If you've taken more than a week to complete the activities, just be sure to add the words to the Wall before moving on to a new packet with its new group of key words.

When we add the words to the wall, it does not mean all students have mastered every word and chunk. Rather, students will continue to practice these words as they reread their favorites and Practice Folders, refer to the Wall during reading and writing, and complete a variety of Word Wall review activities. Constant use of the Wall is key to helping students truly master the words and chunks. You can feel confident about moving on to another poem, rhyme, or chant each week if you plan review time and use your Word Wall continuously (see Use Your Word Wall Every Day, page 16).

I organize the words contained in this book on a "Chunking Wall" in a- e- i- o- u- y- and *other* categories. This is a logical way to organize chunks since they always begin with a vowel. The "other" category is for words with common syllables that are useful to students (like *tion* in *lotion* or *le* in *apple*). Although you can organize your Wall any way you wish, I've found organizing by vowels makes key words easier to find when making analogies to read new words.

Use Your Word Wall Every Day

Be sure to *model* using the Word Wall each day during your reading and writing activities. Show students how they can use a word they know from the Wall to spell or read new words. Think aloud to demonstrate problem solving while writing and reading across many contexts.

For example, while writing, pause and say, "I'm stuck here. What can I do? I'm trying to spell the word *sinking*. I hear /ink/. Oh yes, I know that chunk. It is like *think* on our Chunking Wall. I must need s- i- n- k. I also hear /ing/ like *wing*. I must also need i- n- g. I'm glad I know how to use the Word Wall to help me spell new words!"

Or while reading, "I can't figure out this word. I've thought about what would fit and make sense but I'm still not sure. Let's see. First I see *ut* like *nut* on our Chunking Wall so this must be *shut*. Next I see *er*, the word must be *shutters*. Let me reread to make sure *shutters* make sense here. Looking for chunks and thinking of other words I know that have those chunks really helps me read harder words!"

Also, involve students in lots of Word Wall activities. One of my favorites is "Which Word Would I Use?" I ask students "If I am writing the word *dolphin*, which word from the Wall would help me with the last chunk?" Students then say the word *dolphin* slowly, listening for the final chunk and refer to the Chunking Wall to find the analogous key word. Or I write a challenging word on the board, and ask, "Which words on the Wall would help me read this word?" Students have to chunk the word on the board and find analogous key words on the Wall.

Refer to my book *Teaching Reading and Writing with Word Walls* (Scholastic, 1999) for plenty of ideas for using your Word Wall in meaningful ways every day.

References:

Clay, M. M. (1993). Reading Recovery: *A Guidebook for Teachers in Training*. Portsmouth, NH: Heinemann.

Opitz, M. F. and Ford, M. P. (2001). *Reaching Readers: Flexible and Innovative Strategies for Guided Reading*. Portsmouth, NH: Heinemann.

Wagstaff, J. M. (1999). *Teaching Reading and Writing with Word Walls*. New York: Scholastic.

Wagstaff, J. M. (1994). *Phonics That Work: New Strategies for the Reading/Writing Classroom*. New York: Scholastic.

If You Think You Know This Friend

(Sung to the tune of: "If You're Happy and You Know It")

If you think you know this friend,

shout it out!

If you think you know this friend,

shout it out!

If you think you know this friend,
can you tell me who it is?
If you think you know this friend,

shout it out!

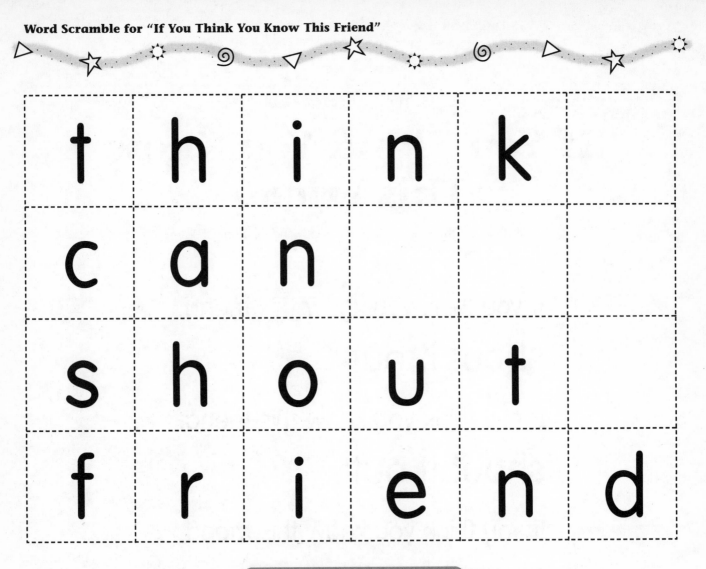

t	h	i	n	k	
c	a	n			
s	h	o	u	t	
f	r	i	e	n	d

If You Think You Know This Friend

Curricular Tie: Beginning of the Year Get To Know You Activities

Use this tune as a springboard for name play at the beginning of the year. Try the following ideas for working on phonological awareness using students' names:

Sing a verse. After each verse give children clues to figure out the name.

* ✳ "This name begins with /b/" (voice the beginning sound of a name).

* ✳ "This name begins like _____" (voice a word that has the same beginning sound as a name).

* ✳ "This name begins with the letter *b*" (say the letter name).

* ✳ "/D/ /e/ /v/ /i/ /n/" (voice all the sounds in a name for students to blend together).

* ✳ "This name rhymes with _____" (say a word that rhymes with the target name).

* ✳ "This name ends with /t/" (voice the ending sound of a name).

* ✳ "This name ends like _____" (say a word that has the same ending sound as the name).

* ✳ "This name has the vowel sound /ee/" (voice the vowel sound of a name).

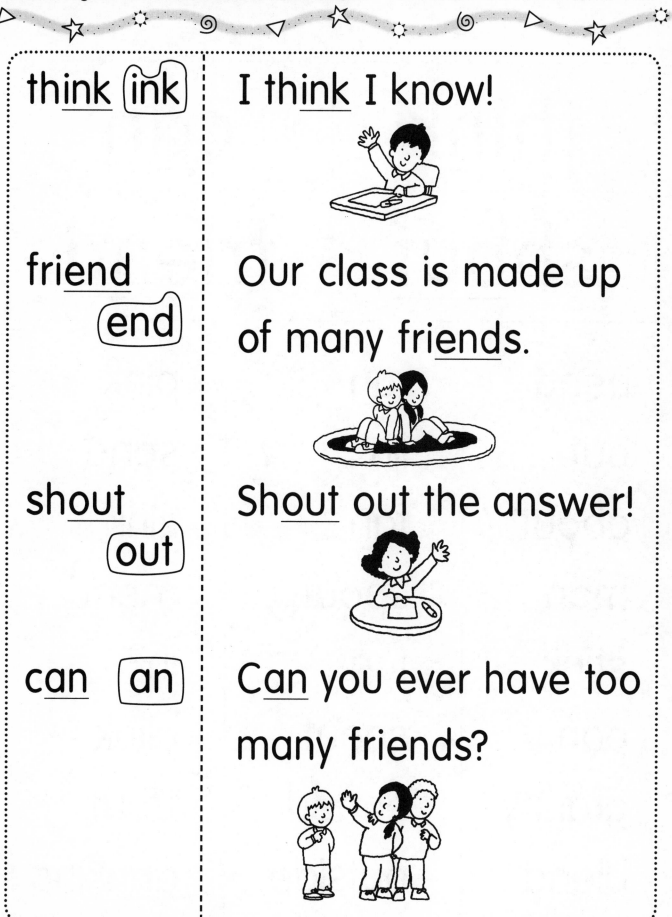

th**ink** **ink**

I th**ink** I know!

fri**end** **end**

Our class is made up of many fri**end**s.

sh**out** **out**

Sh**out** out the answer!

c**an** **an**

C**an** you ever have too many friends?

think	can
shout	friend

bend	ran	pink
out	link	send
about	fan	sink
man	spout	mend
stink	tan	ink
pan	snout	blink
granny	ended	trout
blend	outside	drinking

20 Weekly Word Study Poetry Packets Scholastic Professional Books

Colors

Blue, yellow, red, green,
all the colors can be seen
in the flowers,
in the trees,
in the birds and, yes, the bees.
Purple, orange, black, white
in the sky
and dark, dark night.
What a world of colors here.
Let's give colors a big cheer.
Colors
Colors
Colors
Colors!

t	r	e	e	
d	a	r	k	
w	h	i	t	e
b	l	a	c	k

Colors

Curricular Tie: Art (color identification and mixing); Science (observation in nature); Writing (poetry writing)

Have a great time exploring colors with this poem. At the end, cheer: "Colors, colors, colors, colors!"–getting louder each time. Discuss and experiment with primary and secondary colors. Go on a "I Spy Colors In Nature" walk. Kids take a notepad and pencil and write down the colors they see and their corresponding objects in nature. Students then use their notes to write their own poems about colors.

tree (ee)   Trees give us shade.

dark (ark)   The night is dark.

white (ite)   Clouds are white.

black (ack)   Look at the black hat.

tree   dark

white   black

bark	Jack	bite
bees	kite	sack
park	flee	write
snack	tack	site
knee	shark	glee
shacks	crack	spark
attack	bites	stark
barked	quite	spree
frisbee	packing	

20 Weekly Word Study Poetry Packets Scholastic Professional Books

Take Care of Yourself

Take care of yourself!
You're the only you you've got!
Eat healthy foods and
exercise a lot!
Get lots of sleep
and you'll see your body grow.
Take care of yourself.
Let your best you show!

c	a	r	e
s	l	e	e	p
g	r	o	w
b	e	s	t

TEACHING NOTES

Take Care of Yourself
Curricular Tie: Health

When working with this poem, invite students to think about other ways to maintain a healthy lifestyle. Brainstorm ways to meet the goals already covered in the poem (eat healthy foods, exercise, sleep). For example, list types of healthy foods and allow children to share their favorite exercises with the class.

care (are)   Take care of yourself.

sleep
(eep)   Get some sleep!

grow (ow)   Our bodies grow.

best (est)   Do your best work!

care	sleep
grow	best

dare	beep	rest
blow	deep	crow
share	vest	west
steep	stare	chest
show	creep	flows
lower	zesty	sweep
snowy	nested	peeping
glare	slowest	shared
careful	deeper	mower
festival	sleeping	

20 Weekly Word Study Poetry Packets Scholastic Professional Books

Five Fat Peas

Five fat peas
sittin' in a pod.
One said, "Let's go!"
and left with a nod.
Another rolled away
when the first one went,
leaving only three
in their pea pod tent.
"I'm off," cried the next,
"to see the world!" She dropped.
The one next to her
ejected with a POP!
"Now there's only me,"
said the last lone pea.
"I guess I'd better plant myself
and grow more family!"

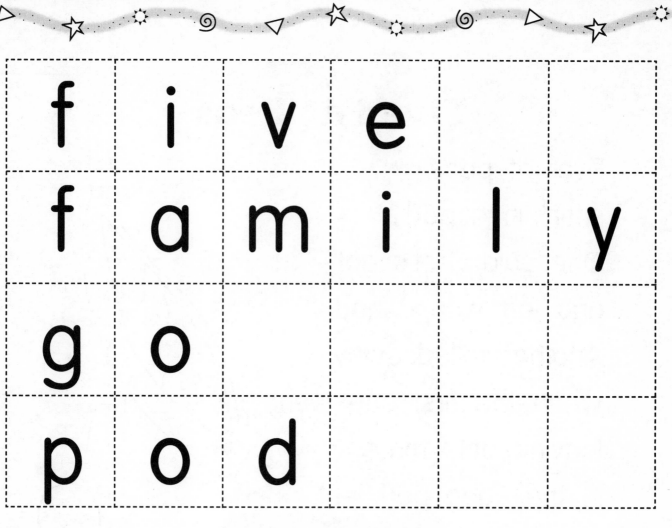

Five Fat Peas

Curricular Tie: Math (subtraction); Drama; Writing Conventions (quotation marks)

This poem is a great way to explore the concept of subtraction in first grade and a super beginning of the year review of the concept in second. Kids love to recite the poem with great expression and act it out in small groups. Another option is to use finger puppets.

If your students are ready, use Wikki-stix or highlighting tape to call attention to the quotation marks on the shared reading poster. Explain how the quotation marks work and determine a type of voice for each speaker. Read and reread the poem using these voices (the sillier the better!).

five | ive

Here are five peas.

pod | od

Peas grow in a pod.

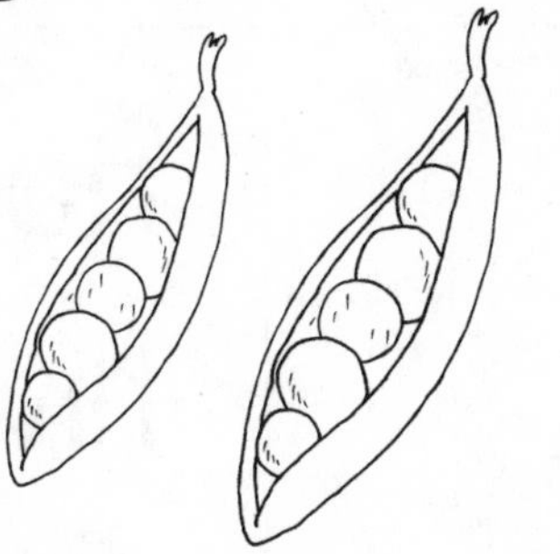

go | o

Let's go!

family | am

A pod holds a family of peas.

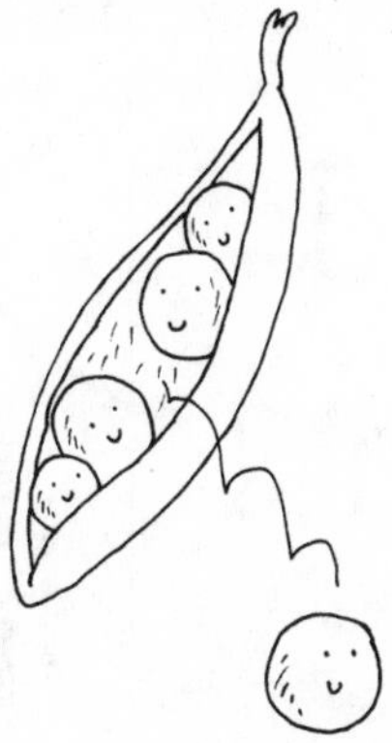

five	family
g**o**	p**o**d

dive	nod	jam
no	hive	rod
live	so	Sam
ham	jive	ho
drive	yo-yo	yam
Flo	alive	sod
model	strive	mam
nodded	going	Pam
mammal	pods	diver
hives	hamburger	

20 Weekly Word Study Poetry Packets Scholastic Professional Books

Winter Months

Winter months,
winter months.
What happens in the
winter months?

Snow and ice,
frost and skis,
some hot chocolate,
if you please?

Holidays and
the New Year, too.
Winter months
bring much to do!

Winter months,
winter months,
I love the
winter months!

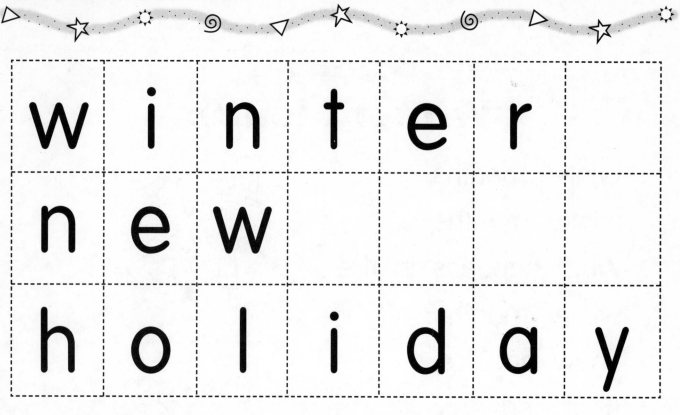

winter

new

holiday

Winter Months

Curricular Tie: Science (seasons); Writing (poetry writing)

Use this poem near the first day of winter to hold a discussion about wintertime weather and activities. Compare winter weather and activities to those of other seasons. Use the pattern in the poem to write other poems for seasons. (Beginning: "Fall months, fall months, What happens in the fall months? . . ." Ending: "Fall months, fall months, I love the fall months!")

winter

in

Winter days are cold.

new ew

Happy New Year!

holiday

ay

What's your favorite holiday?

win<u>t</u>er	n<u>ew</u>
holi<u>day</u>	

pin	few	hay
may	blew	fins
play	win	chew
drew	gray	tray
grin	sway	grew
chin	crew	thin
playing	newer	stew
anyway	spinning	inside
pewter	mayor	stray
thinner	chewing	crayon

20 Weekly Word Study Poetry Packets Scholastic Professional Books

Animal Voices

A duck says "quack"
and a cat says "meow."
What is the sound
you hear from a cow?
A fish goes "blub"
and a snake goes "hiss."
So many animals
too good to miss!

Animal Voices

Curricular Tie: Science

This poem is a great introduction to studying animals with young children. Generate a list of distinguishing animal features (in addition to the sound they make as shown in the poem) and read books to find matches for each one. For example, one characteristic may be animals with fur. Examples might be bears, cats, dogs, and gerbils. Another characteristic may be animals that live in water, and so on.

d<u>uck</u> **uck**	A d<u>uck</u> swims.
f<u>ish</u> **ish**	Feed the f<u>ish</u>.
bl<u>ub</u> **ub**	A fish goes "bl<u>ub</u>!"
h<u>iss</u> **iss**	A snake h<u>iss</u>es.
c<u>at</u> **at**	A c<u>at</u> meows.

f<u>i</u>sh	bl<u>u</u>b
h<u>iss</u>	c<u>at</u>
d<u>uck</u>	

cub	wish	pat
bats	kisses	luck
rub	buck	sub
dishes	chat	fatter
missed	swish	tuck
truck	bliss	splat
hissing	lucky	club
flatten	grub	stuck
struck	dismiss	buckle
bubble	Saturday	fishes

20 Weekly Word Study Poetry Packets Scholastic Professional Books

The 100th Day of School

Wow!

We're here!

100 days

100 days of school!

Watch us shine!

100 ways

100 days! We're cool!

10, 20, 30

Our work has been great!

40, 50, 60

Our skills are first-rate!

70, 80, 90

Learning all the way

to 100!

The 100th,

the 100th school day!

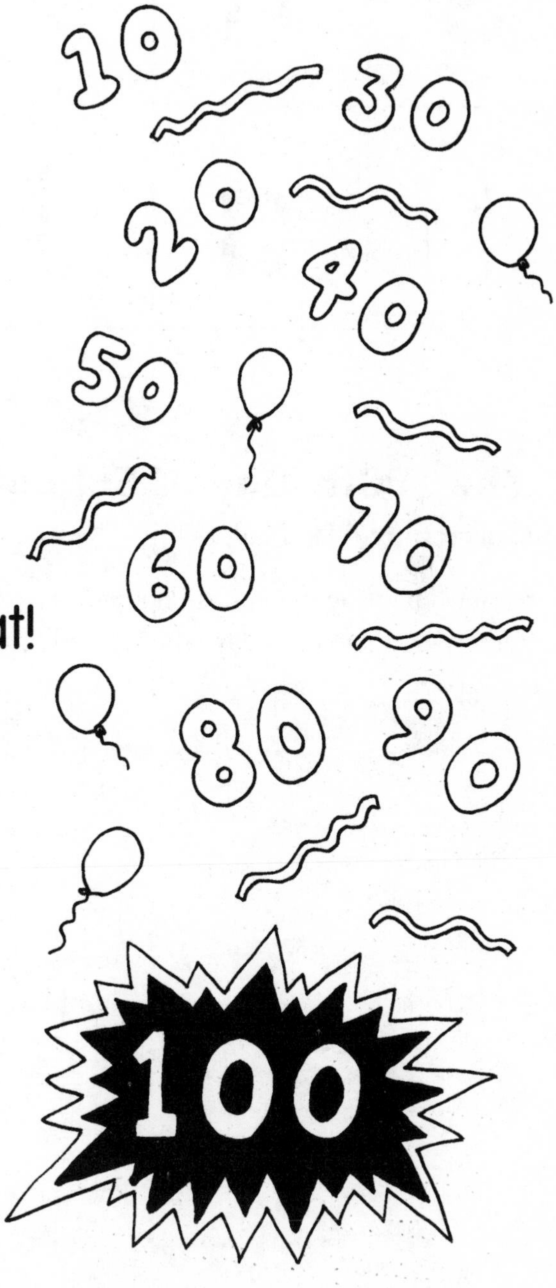

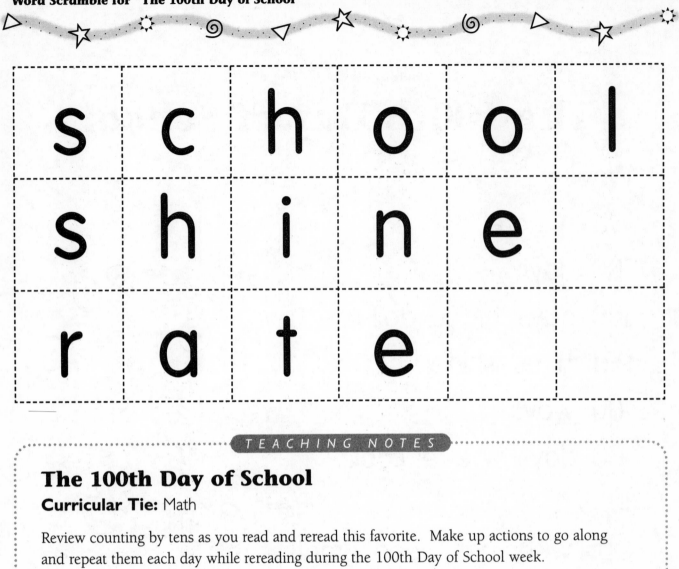

s	c	h	o	o	l
s	h	i	n	e	
r	a	t	e		

The 100th Day of School

Curricular Tie: Math

Review counting by tens as you read and reread this favorite. Make up actions to go along and repeat them each day while rereading during the 100th Day of School week.

school _oo_l

[_ool_]

We learn in school.

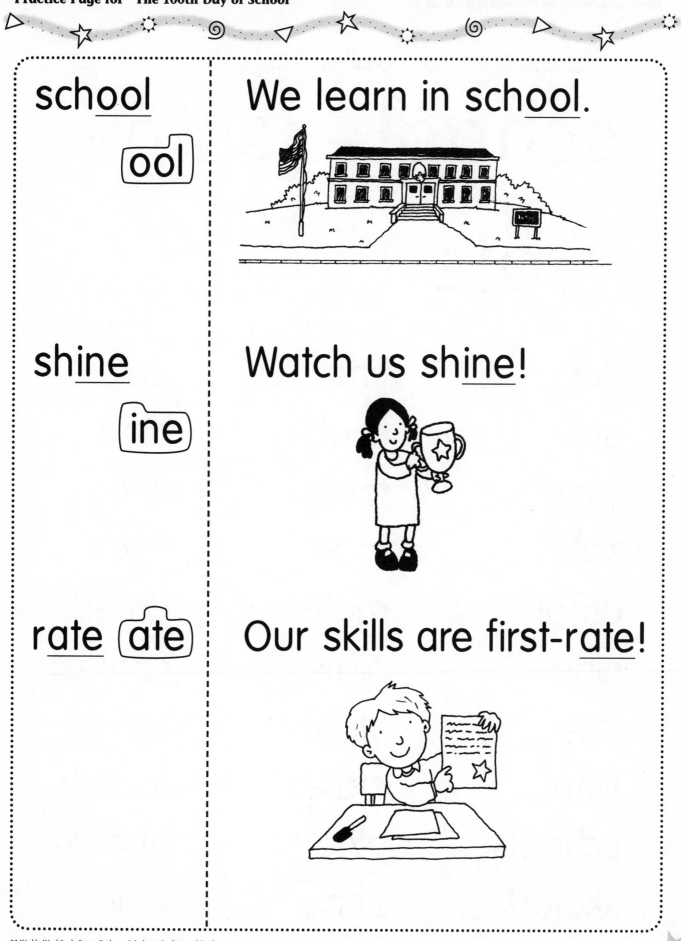

shine

[_ine_]

Watch us sh_ine_!

r_ate_ [_ate_]

Our skills are first-r_ate_!

school	shine
rate	

pool	fine	date
ate	cool	dine
lines	tools	later
Kate	fool	mine
drool	mate	dated
nine	plate	coolest
fate	stool	spine
vine	states	foolish
schools	pine	update
skated	brine	twine

20 Weekly Word Study Poetry Packets Scholastic Professional Books

Stop! And Spot a Tadpole

Stop!

And spot a tadpole,

swimming in a pond.

Notice how he looks,

he's soon to be a frog!

Croaking by a brook

Or sitting on a log!

Ribbit!

s	w	i	m			
b	r	o	o	k		
s	p	o	t			
t	a	d	p	o	l	e

Stop and Spot A Tadpole
Curricular Tie: Science

Use this poem to explore metamorphosis and lifecycles. Visit a local pet store to bring in a tadpole and watch it change over time. Record observations in a learning log. Brainstorm other animals that go through metamorphosis and sketch models of their life cycles. Relate the idea of life cycles to other cycles in nature (like the cycle of the seasons over a year, the cycle of a day, and so on).

swim

im

Tadpoles swim.

brook

ook

Frogs croak by the brook.

spot ot

Did you spot a tadpole?

tadpole

ad

Tadpoles change into frogs.

sw<u>im</u>	br<u>ook</u>
s<u>po</u>t	t<u>ad</u>pole

Jim	lot	book
pot	mad	him
took	rim	sad
bad	cook	hot
shot	Brad	slim
plot	sadder	crook
brim	otter	badly
looked	trimming	shook
hotter	swimmer	gladly
sadly	pottery	nook

20 Weekly Word Study Poetry Packets Scholastic Professional Books

Let's Get the Rhythm

Let's get the rhythm of the game.
(Snap, snap) Now you've got the
rhythm of the game. (Snap, snap)

Let's get the rhythm of the hands.
(Clap, clap) Now you've got the rhythm
of the hands. (Clap, clap)

Let's get the rhythm of the head.
(Shake, shake) Now you've got the
rhythm of the head. (Shake, shake)

Let's get the rhythm of the feet.
(Stamp, stamp) Now you've got the
rhythm of the feet. (Stamp, stamp)

Adapted from Anne Miranda's book *Let's Get The Rhythm* (Scholastic, 1994)

TEACHING NOTES

Let's Get The Rhythm

Work cooperatively to create additional verses and movements for the chant.
For example, "Let's get the rhythm of the knees. (Bend, bend) Now you've got the rhythm of the knees. (Bend, bend)" Add these verses to the shared reading poster for everyone to revisit and enjoy. Don't forget to enjoy the book version of this chant (Ann Miranda, 1994, Scholastic. ISBN: 0590273663)

clap (ap)   Clap your hands.

shake   Shake your head.

(ake)

game   Let's play a game!

(ame)

clap

game

shake

nap	make	name
same	lap	take
rake	came	tap
slap	lake	blame
brake	frame	fake
happy	Blake	snap
shame	apple	stake
awake	blamed	straps
unwrap	mistake	games
framed	trapped	brakes
Japanese	milkshake	named
forsake	tapestry	tamed

20 Weekly Word Study Poetry Packets Scholastic Professional Books

Adding Is Fun

(Sung to the tune of: "The Adams Family")

Adding is fun! Snap, snap!
Adding is fun! Snap, snap!
Adding is fun! Adding is fun!
Adding is fun! Snap, snap!

When I need to add
I start with my ones.
If they're ten or more
I trade that ten right now!

Adding is fun! Snap, snap!
Adding is fun! Snap, snap!
Adding is fun! Adding is fun!
Adding is fun! Snap, snap!

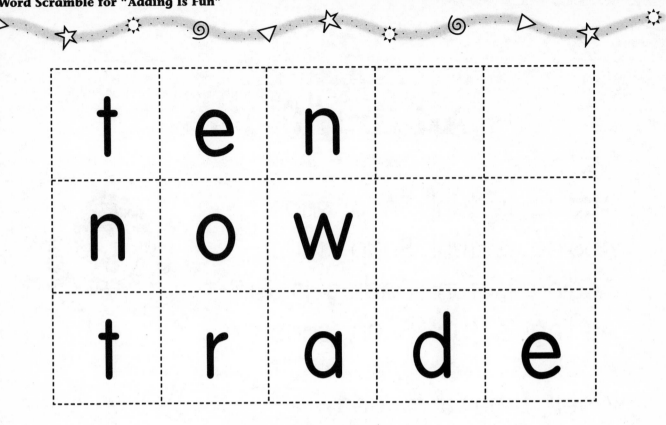

t	e	n		
n	o	w		
t	r	a	d	e

Adding Is Fun
Curricular Tie: Math

This poem provides a wonderful way to help students remember the process of adding with carrying (or trading, as we now call it). Sung to the tune of "The Adams Family," its catchy tune is fun and memorable for kids. Model the process of working addition problems with trading on the overhead while singing the tune. Encourage students to sing the tune to themselves when they get stuck working a problem.

t<u>en</u>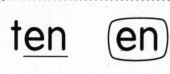

Т<u>en</u> ones make one t<u>en</u>. $1+1+1+1+1+$ $1+1+1+1+1=10$

tr<u>ade</u>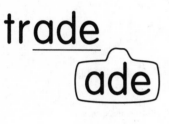

You must tr<u>ade</u> ten ones for one ten.

n<u>ow</u> ow

What time is it n<u>ow</u>?

ten	trade
now	

fade	cow	hen
wow	pen	made
blades	how	chow
den	then	flower
shower	Jenny	vows
when	trader	wade
power	arcade	energy
waded	enlarge	shades
showered	parade	bowing
invade	towel	dentist
chowder	eyebrow	remade
stencil	envelope	lemonade
empower	entrance	escapade

20 Weekly Word Study Poetry Packets Scholastic Professional Books

When You Need To Subtact

(Sung to the tune of: "Mary Had a Little Lamb")

When you need to subtract,
to subtract,
to subtract,
when you need to subtract
look at your ones!
If you have enough ones on top,
enough ones on top,
enough ones on top,
if you have enough ones on top,
just subtract!
If there aren't enough ones on top,
enough ones on top,
enough ones on top,
trade a ten and add ten ones.
Then you can subtract!

s	u	b	t	r	a	c	t
j	u	s	t				
t	o	p					
e	n	o	u	g	h		

TEACHING NOTES

When You Need to Subtract

Curricular Tie: Math; Writing

I experienced such success using the "Adding Is Fun" tune with addition, I decided to create a tune for subtraction with borrowing (or trading). "When You Need To Subtract" is sung to the tune of "Mary Had A Little Lamb." Model the process of working subtraction problems with trading on the overhead while singing the tune. Encourage students to sing the tune to themselves when they get stuck working a problem.

As a fun extension after using "Adding Is Fun" and "When You Need To Subtract," invite students to create their own rendition of a math concept by adapting the lyrics of a familiar tune.

subtract

act

Do you know how to subtract?

$$4 - 2 = \_$$

just   ust

Wait just a minute!

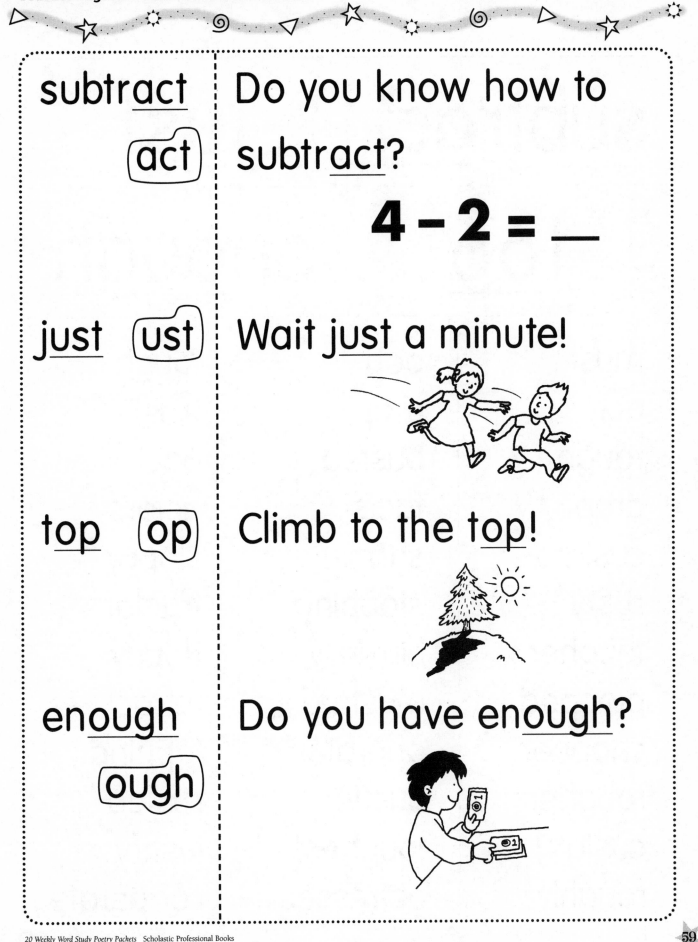

top   op

Climb to the top!

enough

ough

Do you have enough?

subtract	just
top	enough

must	pop	tough
act	mop	trust
rough	busted	pact
drop	facts	actors
custard	shops	sloppy
rusty	stopping	tractor
tougher	blustery	floppy
plopped	mustard	retract
chopper	operator	topping
rougher	bustle	rusted
custard	toughest	justify
roughly	actresses	cooperate

20 Weekly Word Study Poetry Packets Scholastic Professional Books

Precipitation

Pit

pat

pit

pat

rain is falling.

Puddles gather.

Drift

sway

float

twist

snow is falling.

Tracks in white.

Bish

boom

crack

smack

hail is falling.

Ice balls jump.

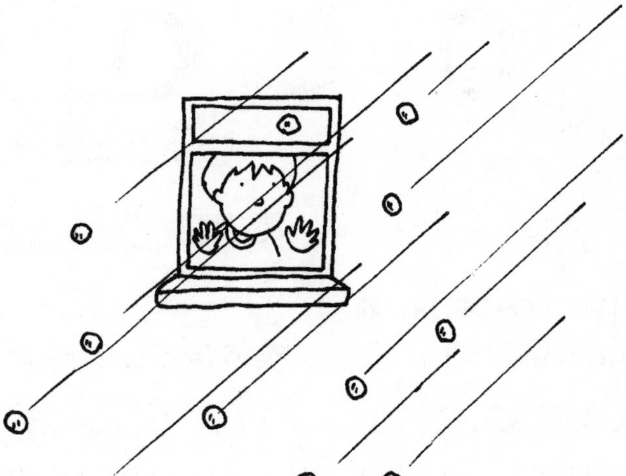

All are types of precipitation.

What kind comes down in your location?

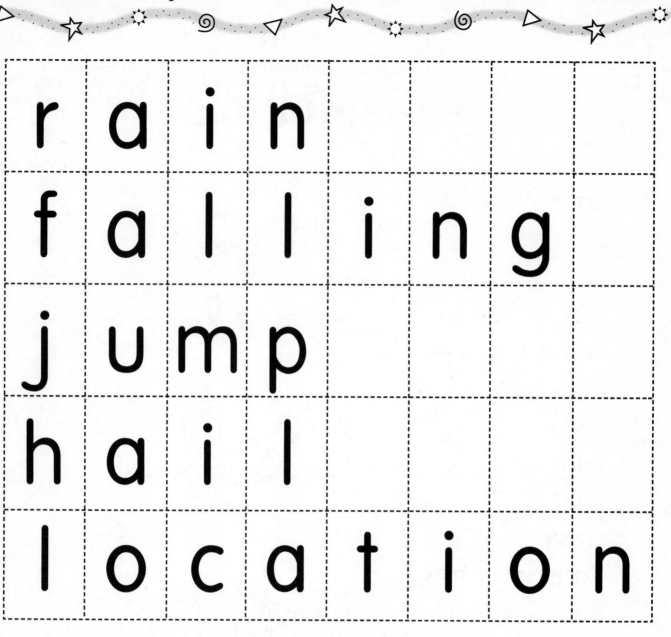

r a i n				
f a l l i n g				
j u m p				
h a i l				
l o c a t i o n				

Precipitation

Curricular Tie: Science; Math (measurement); Writing

Use this poem as a springboard for exploring all types of weather. Brainstorm other forms of precipitation. Set up a collection station outside your classroom for measuring amounts of precipitation. With older students, explore weather trends across the globe (like climates at the equator and the poles).

Use the language in the poem to study onomatopoeia. Share the pen to record other words that sound like their referents—*buzz, bash, cuckoo*. Model writing your own onomatopoetic poem and encourage the students to also give it a try.

rain (ain)   It rains a lot in spring.

falling (all)   Rain is falling.

hail (ail)   Hail is falling.

jump (ump)   Hail jumps when it hits the ground.

location (tion)   I wonder which location gets the most rain?

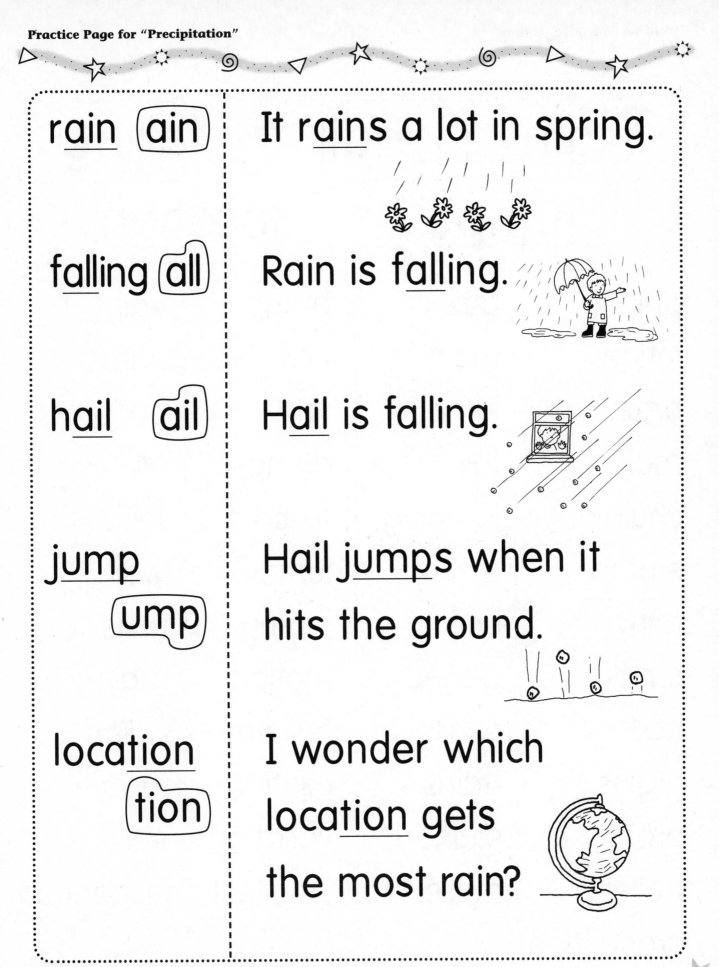

rain	hail	falling
jump		location

pain	ball	bump	sail
lotion	main	pail	hump
brain	lump	tall	potion
mall	tail	dump	all
chain	jumping	fallen	fail
stump	stain	lumpy	wall
rainy	bail	plump	nails
small	grumpy	motion	main
trail	snails	hallway	called
grains	trains	caution	taller
brain	stained	vacation	stall
trailer	mailed	smallest	inspection
graduation			

A Brand-new Year

A brand-new year is here!
I promise to be neat
and do all my chores
I'll even wash my feet!

A brand-new year is here!
Making goals is swell.
I promise to eat vegetables
and clear my plate, as well.

A brand-new year is here!
I'll even wash the car,
do my homework, get good grades,
earn that gold star!

A brand-new year is here!
Oh, gee, I'm getting weary.
Maybe all these things can wait
'till next January!

b	r	a	n	d
y	e	a	r	
g	o	l	d	
s	w	e	l	l
n	e	a	t	

A Brand-new Year

Curricular Tie: Social Studies

Use this poem to get your new year started with a bang! Encourage students to generate their own goals—one for school and one for home. Record the goals on a class chart. Have students record their goals on paper and attach a magnet for a reminder on their refrigerator at home. Discuss the steps needed to reach goals.

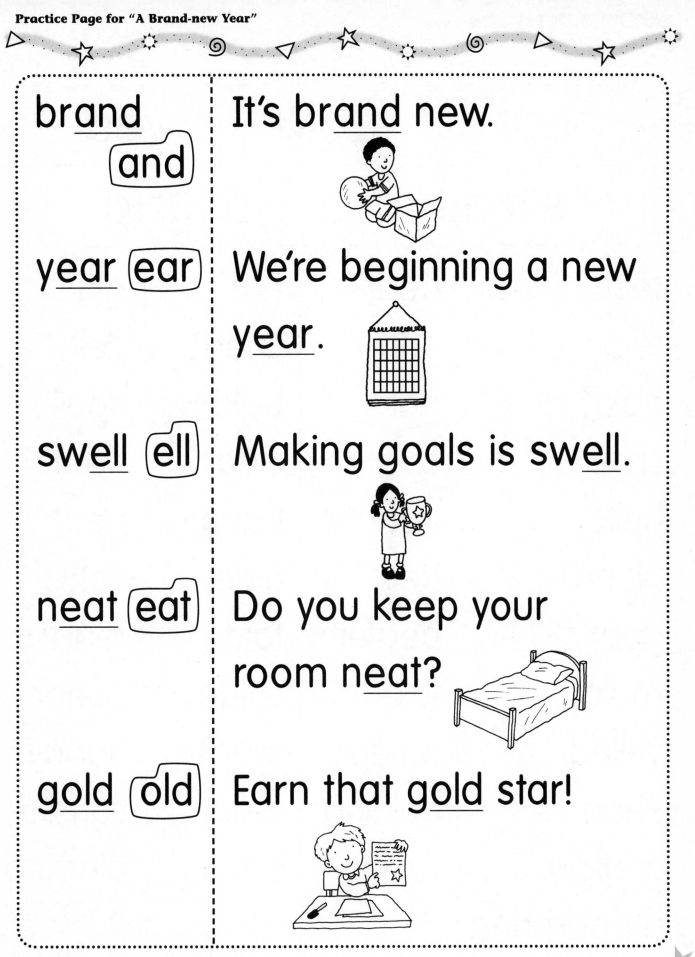

brand **and**

year **ear**

swell **ell**

neat **eat**

gold **old**

It's brand new.

We're beginning a new year.

Making goals is swell.

Do you keep your room neat?

Earn that gold star!

neat	gold	year

swell	brand

fell	dear	eat	old
tear	sand	cheat	tell
hold	ears	bold	spell
smell	cold	clear	beat
hello	hearing	band	neat
bland	bells	older	sold
gear	beater	fold	fearful
moldy	told	coldest	spear
yelled	eaten	smelly	handy
shear	holding	yellow	candle
mellow	folder	earring	pleated
rubberband			

20 Weekly Word Study Poetry Packets Scholastic Professional Books

Earthland

Let's hear a cheer
for Mother Earth,
place where we live,
place of our birth.
Protect her forests
and her oceans.
Protect her animals,
show devotion.
If we let them die,
you see,
We lose some of
Earth's family.
So raise a cheer
and lift a hand!
Pay tribute to
this great Earthland!

c	h	e	e	r
p	l	a	c	e
l	i	f	t	
l	e	t		
f	a	m	i	l	y

Earthland

Curricular Tie: Social Studies (civic responsibility); Science

After reading this poem and discussing the issues associated with Earth Day, develop your own class project to help the Earth. This might be as simple as organizing a schoolyard cleanup. Read a variety of Earth Day related books to help your students generate ideas (*50 Simple Things Kids Can Do To Save The Earth* (Scholastic, 1990; ISBN # 0-590-44249-X) and *Save The Earth* (Troll Associates, 1992; ISBN # 0-8167-2580-2) are great places to start).

cheer
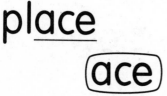

Shout out a cheer!

place

What is your favorite place?

lift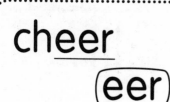

Lift a hand to help the Earth.

let

Let's pitch in and help.

family

Animals are part of the Earth's family.

place	let	lift

cheer	family

gift	pet	slowly
races	jeer	lace
met	ugly	nets
swift	deer	vet
grace	sadly	bet
fret	trace	drift
peer	rift	veer
misplace	getting	better
sneer	faced	softly
wettest	embrace	steers
nearly	fifty	regret
cheerful	swifter	hardly
misplace	unhappily	letters

20 Weekly Word Study Poetry Packets Scholastic Professional Books

Safety, Safety

Safety, safety,
that's what I say!
When you cross the street
look both ways!
Don't talk to strangers
'cause some are bad.
Buckle up in the car,
you may wish you had!
Know how to say
"No!" to drugs.

Choose good friends
don't hang with thugs!
Don't play with matches,
leave guns alone.
Don't give out info
on the phone.

Know the safety rules.
These are a few.
I know more.
How 'bout you?

c	a	r					
c	r	o	s	s			
m	a	t	c	h	e	s	
s	t	r	a	n	g	e	r
b	u	c	k	l	e		

TEACHING NOTES

Safety, Safety

Curricular Tie: Social Studies; Writing

Students are challenged at the end of this poem to generate other safety rules. After doing so, role-play situations to allow them to practice safety rules. Make your own "Big Book of Safety" by writing each rule on poster paper for volunteers to illustrate.

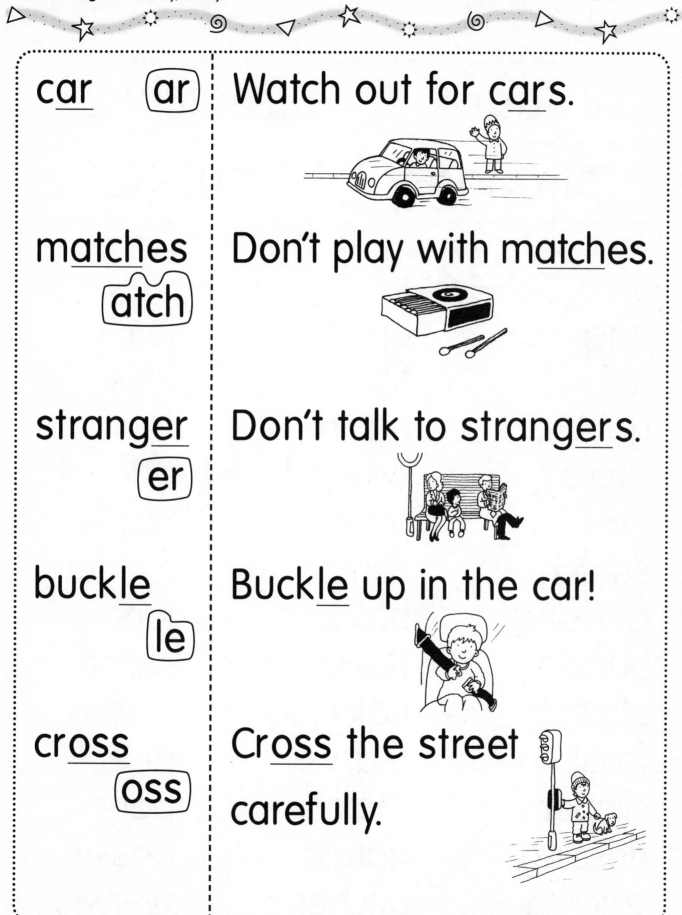

car   ar   Watch out for cars.

matches   Don't play with matches.
atch

stranger   Don't talk to strangers.
er

buckle   Buckle up in the car!
le

cross   Cross the street
oss   carefully.

car	matches
strang**er**	buck**le**
cr**oss**	

boss	apple	latch
her	far	loss
gobble	patch	fatter
mossy	wiper	bar
tar	gloss	pickle
snatch	candle	feeder
crossing	batch	jars
bundle	floss	sister
stars	hatching	tosses
fossil	marvel	needle
slipper	thatch	parlor
flossing	gargle	bossy
catches	pitcher	twinkle

Signs of Spring

Signs of spring
all around,
plants sprouting
from the ground.
Baby animals
lick new fur.
Eggs hatch,
insects stir.
Trees are filled
with budding leaves,
we enjoy a
nice spring breeze.
Warmer weather
is such fun
after winter's
lack of sun.
Fly a kite
or climb a tree!
Celebrate
spring with me!

n	i	c	e
s	u	n	
g	r	o	u	n	d
f	i	l	l	e	d
e	n	j	o	y

Signs of Spring
Curricular Tie: Science; Art

Go outside for a spring walk and look for additional signs of spring. Pick a favorite sign of spring and watercolor a picture to show this sign. Share the pictures with the class, challenging classmates to guess each sign of spring depicted.

My favorite spring book related to signs of spring is : *Springtime* by Ann Schweninger (Scholastic, 1993; ISBN # 0-590-61745-1). This book is one in a series by Schweninger covering all the seasons. They are all excellent resources.

ground
ound

Plants come from the gr<u>ound</u>.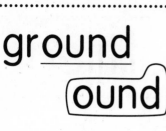

filled ill

I am f<u>ill</u>ed with happiness when spring comes.

nice ice

Flowers are n<u>ice</u>.

enjoy oy

I enj<u>oy</u> springtime activities.

sun un

The s<u>un</u> warms us.

nice	sun	filled
ground		enjoy

toy	fun	will	rice
found	hill	run	boy
twice	bound	Bill	runs
joy	mice	bun	sill
funny	ahoy	pound	price
running	spill	boys	slice
chilly	sounded	illness	still
annoy	under	nicer	spills
mound	enjoyed	sunny	boys
priced	grounded	hundred	spilling
employ	rebound	entice	thunder
thrilling	miller	employee	

20 Weekly Word Study Poetry Packets Scholastic Professional Books

Seeds! Oh, Seeds!

Seeds! Oh, seeds!
So much inside!
Trees, flowers,
plants far and wide,
fruits and vegetables
like carrots for you,
food for us, animals,
insects, too.

Trees give us shelter
with their wood,
bugs live in plant-iful
neighborhoods.
Without them
living things would starve
or lack shelter
to save them from harm.

Think of the power
packed into a seed,
sprouting and growing
to fulfill our needs—
even enriching the
air that we breathe.
Powerful, plentiful, plant-iful seeds!

s	h	e	l	t	e	r
s	a	v	e			
l	i	k	e			
s	e	e	d			

TEACHING NOTES

Seeds! Oh Seeds!

Curricular Tie: Science; Writing

Ask students to bring in a variety of seed packets. Create a "seed examination station" where students examine the seeds in the packets and record similarities and differences. Plant the seeds to create your own class garden. (I've used an outdoor plastic pool (the kind made for toddlers) to do this inside the classroom.)

Brainstorm other benefits of plants beyond those listed in the poem.

You might also use this poem to examine the use of alliteration (*powerful, plentiful, plant-iful* seeds) and language play (bugs live in *plant-iful* neighborhoods).

Clarifying note: Explain to students the idea behind the phrase "even enriching the air that we breathe:" All plants take in carbon dioxide and give off oxygen thus supporting all animal life!

shelter elt

We all need shelter.

save ave

Save some space in your yard for a garden.

like ike

Do you like fruits and vegetables?

seed eed

I plant seeds every spring.

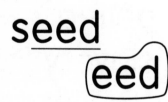

shelter	save
seed	like

bike	gave	Dave
belt	hike	need
pave	weed	wave
bleed	rave	Mike
melt	feeds	alike
greed	cave	grave
breed	bleeding	felt
seedling	knelt	pelted
needy	brave	slavery
hiker	shave	swelter
engrave	melted	likeness
greedy	dislike	speeding
caveman	bravery	

Insects, Insects

Insects, insects,
do you know?
Look! Three body parts
on the go!

Watch them crawl
or scurry or fly
on six legs
or wings in sky.

Hatched from eggs,
eating plants or each other.
Some are fighters!
Would you eat your brother?

Some have stingers
or suck with long tongues.
Some make their homes
with their own dung!

Insects, insects,
now you know!
Go outside and
watch the show!

p	a	r	t			
w	i	n	g			
p	l	a	n	t		
f	i	g	h	t	e	r
o	u	t	s	i	d	e

TEACHING NOTES

Insects, Insects

Curricular Tie: Science; Reading; Writing

After studying insect body parts, have students create their own imaginative models of insects with geometric pattern blocks from your math curriculum. The only rule is that the models must be true to insect form (three body parts, six legs). Read books about insects to find examples of the behaviors described in the poem (Find examples of plant-eating insects, cannibalistic insects, fighting insects, and so on.) After doing this research, create a class book of insect riddles (such as, Who sucks with a long tongue?, and so forth).

You might have a hard time finding the insect that builds its home with its own dung. This is a type of caterpillar which builds a tunnel like structure for a home using its own dung. YUCK!

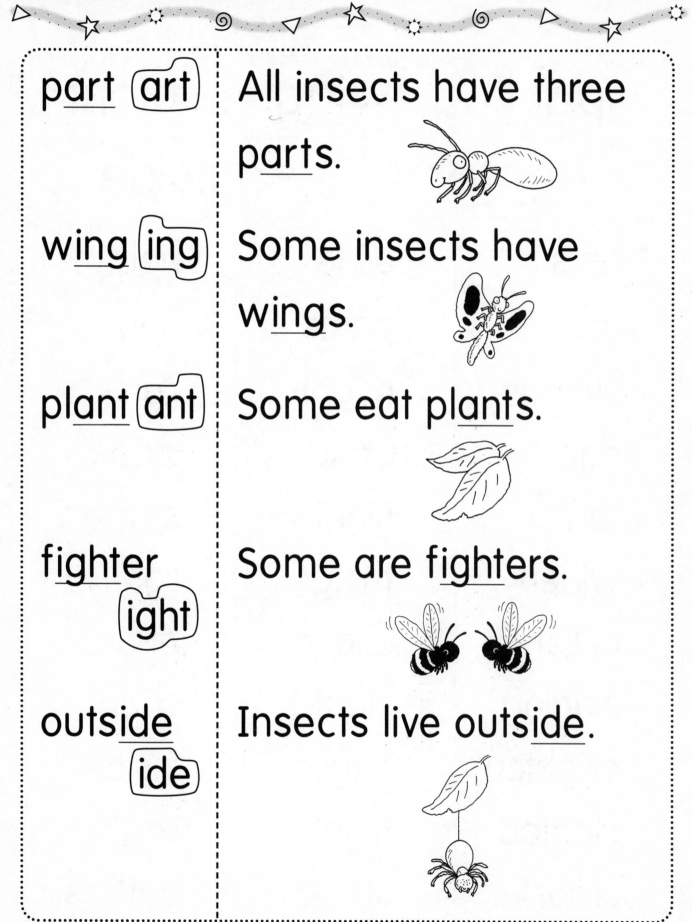

part art   All insects have three parts.

wing ing   Some insects have wings.

plant ant   Some eat plants.

fighter ight   Some are fighters.

outside ide   Insects live outside.

part	wing	plant
fighter		outside

ants	glide	right
art	pants	ring
swings	might	carts
ride	bring	sides
rant	sight	started
wider	things	lightly
artist	charts	pride
singing	slant	chant
brighten	finger	inside
slanted	flight	jingle
smarter	stride	antlers

20 Weekly Word Study Poetry Packets Scholastic Professional Books

Parenthood

Have you ever seen
a bear cub
fishing with its mother?
Have you ever seen
a kitten
sucking milk with a brother?
Have you ever seen
a bird parent
feeding a baby chick?
Have you ever seen
a mother lion
give her cub a lick?
Have you ever seen
a mother whale
push her baby topside?
Have you ever seen
a mom kangaroo
take joey for a ride?
Have you ever seen
a small bat-ling
cling to mother's chest?
Have you ever seen
a baby bird
mouth open in a nest?
Mammals and birds,
have you heard?
Care for their young.
I'd much rather be
one of these
than alone from day one!

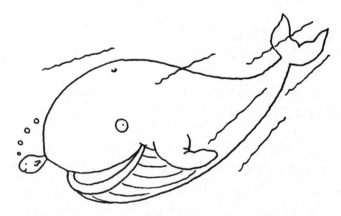

k	i	t	t	e	n
p	a	r	e	n	t
b	a	b	y		
c	h	i	c	k	
w	h	a	l	e	

TEACHING NOTES

Parenthood

Curricular Tie: Science

Explore the categories of vertebrate animals (fish, birds, mammals, amphibians and reptiles), listing the characteristics of each group. Ask students to bring in plastic animals to categorize.

Discuss how, in general, only mammals and birds care for their young. Have students flip through magazines to cut out pictures of animals to categorize according to how they are cared for. Divide a piece of poster paper into columns labeled: no parent, one parent, two parents, groups. Paste the magazine pictures in the appropriate columns.

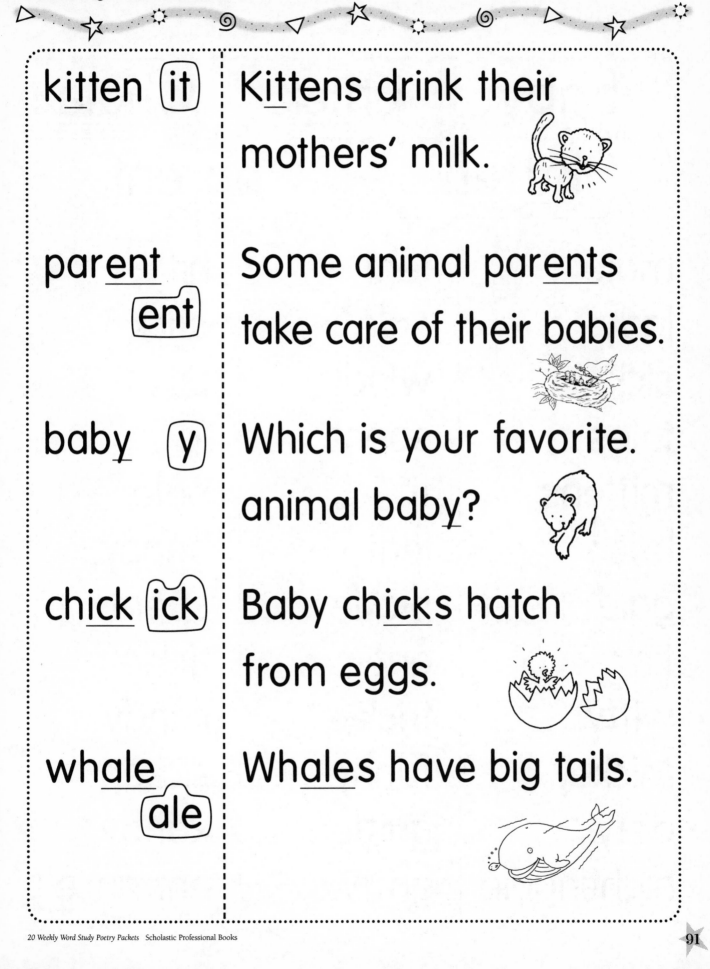

ki<u>tt</u>en **it**	Ki<u>tt</u>ens drink their mothers' milk.
par<u>ent</u> **ent**	Some animal par<u>ent</u>s take care of their babies.
bab<u>y</u> **y**	Which is your favorite. animal bab<u>y</u>?
chi<u>ck</u> **ick**	Baby chi<u>ck</u>s hatch from eggs.
wh<u>ale</u> **ale**	Wh<u>ale</u>s have big tails.

baby	chick	whale

kitten	parent

male	tent	hit
lady	sale	stick
sick	windy	bit
tales	spent	Rick
mittens	fit	pale
brick	lent	happy
gale	pickle	spent
tiny	grit	tickle
witty	trickle	candy
Mickey	funny	sicken
dirty	quitter	Randy
nightingale	gritty	entrance

20 Weekly Word Study Poetry Packets Scholastic Professional Books

I'm a Scientist

I ask questions
'cause that's what scientists do.
When I want to find out
I use observation, too.
I try this and that
and write down what I see.
Keeping track of data
is important to me.
Then I have to think,
"What does all this mean?"
Drawing a conclusion
means explaining what I've seen.
I'm proud to be a scientist,
doing what scientists do.
Come with me, and you'll see....
You'll want to be one, too!

f	i	n	d		
a	s	k			
d	o	w	n		
s	e	e	n		
d	r	a	w	i	n	g

I'm A Scientist

Curricular Tie: Science

Use this poem to clearly outline the steps in the scientific process. Create a chart depicting the steps:

* Form a hypothesis (ask a question)

* Investigate (run tests) (try this and that)

* Record data

* Examine results (what does all this mean?)

* Draw a conclusion

Refer to the chart whenever doing class demonstrations of science experiments. Encourage students to use the scientific vocabulary when writing about their experiences in their learning logs.

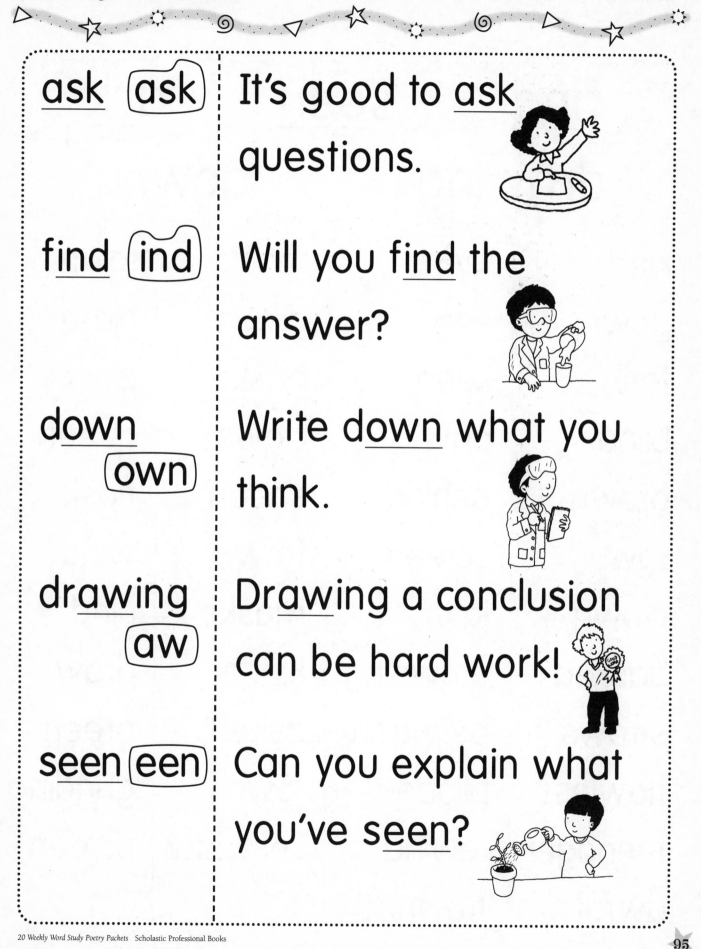

ask ask   It's good to ask questions.

find ind   Will you find the answer?

down own   Write down what you think.

drawing aw   Drawing a conclusion can be hard work!

seen een   Can you explain what you've seen?

find	seen	ask

drawing	down

kind	teen	mask	town
gown	saw	green	mind
task	keen	bask	clown
blind	paw	claws	queen
brown	behind	sheen	flask
raw	screen	frown	wind
crown	jaw	masks	hind
basked	drowning	kinder	draw
straws	between	asked	preen
flawless	blinded	towns	grinding
teenager	rewind	coleslaw	screen
awful	frowned		

20 Weekly Word Study Poetry Packets Scholastic Professional Books